NEW INDIA: MISSION 2020 AND THE COVID-19 U-TURN

DR. ABUL KALAM AJAD

Contents

CHAPTER ONE

INTRODUCTION

Our motherland India is a land of great wealth and potential. At the same time, it is also a country of poverty, illiteracy, backwardness and ignorance. India is a land of differences and diversities. There are many languages, cultures, customs, traditions and so on. There are also geographical diversities like plains, mountains, low lands, deserts and thick jungles. But it is important to remember that our country India is an undivided country with all the differences and diversities. It stands united on the principles of Unity in Diversity.

CHAPTER TWO

OLD INDIA VS NEW INDIA

Old India was a country with considerable educational development and having universities, which attracted many students from foreign countries. Chinese students were attracted to the Indian universities, since they offered instruction in the teachings of Buddha.

Ancient India is the Indian sub-continent from pre-historic times to the start of Medieval India, which is typically dated (when the term is still used) to the end of the Gupta Empire around 500 CE. Depending on context, the term Ancient India might cover the modern-day countries of Afghanistan, Sri Lanka, Bangladesh, India, Nepal and Pakistan, though these territories had large cultural differences.

India, the land of diversity, has seen and felt immeasurable winds of change over the years, some of these changes are good, while others are not so good.

India has indeed come off the age and has finally caught up with the modern facets that make the world go around now-a-days.

India has experienced a significant shift in cultural, social and economical aspects of life in the last couple of decades.

Old India was obviously more caste based and family or tribe based. In the times when those social structures were developed, they served valuable purposes. But in the new India, they can be hindrances.

CHAPTER THREE

CHAPTER FOUR

INDIA 75

On 15 August 2022, India celebrated its 75th Independence Day. The Government of India has initiated a national campaign 'Azadi Ka Amrit Mahotsav'. People across the nation will host the national flag at their homes on the occasion and participate in 'Har Ghar Tiranga' campaign.

Various events are being organized under 'Azadi Ka Amrit Mahotsav' by the government. People from all over the country are also being felicitated under the program for their contribution to the country. The day is meant to be celebrated as well as to remember and pay tribute to those who gave up their lives to protect our motherland.

India became independent on 15th August 1947. Before that India was under the British rule for almost two centuries since 1757. The famous freedom fighters includes Rani Lakshmi Bhai of Jhansi, Mahatma Gandhi, Subhash Chandra Bose, Bhagat Singh, Khudiram Bose, Jawaharlal Nehru and so on.

The first war of independence began in 1857. In the 20th century, Mahatma Gandhi led the popular movement for independence. The major movements launched by Gandhi are Non-Co-operation Movement (1920), Civil Disobedience Movement (1930) and Quit India Movement

(1942).

The Indian Constitution, which is the longest written constitution of the world was completed on 26 November 1949. It took the Constituent Assembly 2 years 11 months and 18 days to complete the Constitution who has been drafting it since 1946. On 26th January 1950, the Indian Constitution came into force.

When India became independent in 1947, Jawaharlal Nehru became its first Prime Minister. Nehru was also the Foreign Minister of India. Some of the foreign policies of Nehru were non-alignment, friendly relation with all the country, panchsheel and so on. Nehru believed that through these policies, the world peace could be permanently established.

Nehru also established the Parliamentary form of government in India. Nehru signed the first constitution of Independent India in 1949. Indian Constitution has the uniqueness of being the world's longest written democratic constitution with 395 Articles, 22 parts and 8 schedules. At present, it has 395 Articles, 25 parts and 12 schedules. The objective resolution put forwarded by Nehru became the Preamble of the Indian Constitution.

Nehru was in favour of the Russian model of development and therefore argued in favour of a Socialist economy. The Fundamental Duties were also added by the 42nd Amendment whose concept has been borrowed from the USSR.

After India's independence, Sardar Vallabhbhai Patel, India's first Home Minister took the task of integrating more than 500 princely states that existed within the Indian sub-continent. It was one of the most remarkable work done by Patel.

India has adopted the policies like democracy and secularism to deal with all such kinds of differences and diversities. The election of Dr. Zakir Hussein, Fakuruddin Ali Ahmed, Giani Zail Singh and Dr. APJ Abdul Kalam as the President of India and Dr. Manmohan Singh as the Prime Minister of India are the examples of Secularism in India.

Today India is also emerging as a major power in the world. India has also taken pride steps in advancement in the fields of Science and Technology. In 1969, the Indian Space Research Organisation (ISRO) was formed. In 1974, India first tested its nuclear device. In 1998, India successfully tested five nuclear weapons in Pokhran. India also adopts the policy and promotion of the peaceful use of atomic energy and no first use of nuclear weapons.

CHAPTER FIVE

THE COVID-19 PANDEMIC

Coronavirus disease 2019 (COVID-19) is an infectious disease caused by severe acute respiratory syndrome coronavirus 2 (SARS-COV-2). The disease was first identified in 2019 in Wuhan, the capital of China's Hubei province, and has since spread globally, resulting in the 2019-2020 coronavirus pandemic. Common symptoms include fever, cough, and shortness of breath. Other symptoms may include muscle pain, sputum production, diarrhoea, sore throat, abdominal pain, and loss of smell or taste. While the majority of cases result in mild symptoms, some progress to pneumonia and multi-organ failure. As of March 25, 2020, the overall rate of deaths per number of diagnosed cases is 4.5 percent; ranging from 0.2 percent to 15 percent according to age group and other health problems. The virus is mainly spread during close contact and via respiratory droplets produced when people cough or sneeze. Respiratory droplets may be produced during breathing but the virus is not considered airborne. People may also catch COVID-19 by touching a contaminated surface and then their face. It is more contagious when people are symptomatic, although spread may be possible before symptoms appear. The virus can live on surfaces up to 72 hours. Time from exposure to onset of symptoms is generally between two and fourteen days, with an average of five days. The standard method of diagnosis is by five days. The standard method of diagnosis is by reverse transcription polymerase chain reaction (rRTPCR) from a nasopharyngeal swab. The infection can also be diagnosed from a combination of symptoms, risk factors and a chest CT scan showing features of pneumonia.

Recommended measures to prevent infection include frequent hand washing, social distancing (maintaining physical distance from others, especially from those with symptoms), covering coughs and sneezes with a tissue or inner elbow, and keeping unwashed hands away from the face. The use of masks is recommended by some national health authorities for those who suspect they have the virus and their caregivers, but not for the general public, although simple cloth masks may be use by those who desire them. There is no vaccine or specific antiviral treatment for COVID-19. Management involves treatment of symptoms, supportive care, isolation and experimental measures.

The World Health Organisation (WHO) declared the 2019-2020 coronavirus outbreak a Public Health Emergency of International Concern (PHEIC) on 30 January 2020 and a pandemic on 11 March 2020. Local transmission of the disease has been recorded in many countries across all six WHO regions. Most people infected with the COVID-19 virus will experience mild to moderate respiratory illness and recover without requiring special treatment. Older people, and those with underlying medical problems like cardiovascular disease, diabetes, chronic respiratory disease and cancer are more likely to develop serious illness. The best way to prevent and slow down transmission is be well informed about the COVID-19 virus, the disease it causes and how it spreads. Protect yourself and others from infection by washing your hands or using an alcohol based rub frequently and not touching your face. The COVID-19 virus spreads primarily through droplets of saliva or discharge from the nose when an infected person coughs or sneezes, so it's important that you also practice respiratory etiquette (for example, by coughing into a flexed elbow).

At this time, there are no specific vaccines or treatments for COVID-19. However, there are many ongoing clinical trials evaluating potential treatments. WHO will continue to provide updated information as soon as clinical findings become available. COVID-19 is thought to have originated in a seafood market where wildlife was sold illegally. On February 7, 2020, Chinese researchers said the virus could have spread from an infected animal to humans through illegally trafficked pangolins, prized in Asia for food and medicine. Scientists have pointed to either bats or snakes as possible sources.

At the height of the COVID-19 pandemic's first wave in the mid-2020, we were living the first phase of the COVID-19 virus. It was a relatively new virus and a public health crisis which left governments scrambling to lockdown and the public sector in different countries of the world largely failed. At present, the vaccines for the COVID-19 are out and we are in the second phase of the pandemic. Vaccines for the coronavirus, some using innovative mRNA techniques and developed by international teams have begun rolling out which we had never seen before. The death rates has decreased to a certain extent and new and cheaper tests are being developed each month. As we have entered the second phase of the crisis, which will be led by the dynamism, innovation and competence of the private sector. There are still challenges of distribution of the vaccine due to the huge overcrowded population in our country. But on the horizon, a true post-pandemic world is now in sight. The private sector has delivered the vaccines, but we should not forget the indispensable role that the state played in funding vaccine research and development at a fast speed. Only in East Asia and a few other countries of the world, we have seen an effective public and private sector response. With the exception of a stressed financial sector, India went into the coronavirus crisis with sound economic fundamentals. The lockdown in response to the threat of the virus created unprecedented friction in transactions between buyers and sellers of goods and services as well as of inputs. The lockdown has created a lot of difficulties specially for the backward classes people.

CHAPTER SIX

COVID-19 AND INDIA

Though India has done well in containing the spread of the virus, the vulnerability that India faces is still high. As currently, nearly more than 100 cases have been reported all across India. COVID-19 is spread via airborne droplets (sneeze or cough) or contact with the surface. It is possible that a person can get COVID-19 by touching their own nose, eyes or mouth.

India is highly vulnerable due to the large population constantly travelling and working in urban agglomerations like Delhi-NCR and Mumbai. Public hygiene in India is poor despite the Swachh Bharat Abhiyan (Clean India Movements). As we grapple with the global COVID-19 anxiety and fear, unfortunately, people tend to rely on social media platforms where rumours spread faster than the virus. The United Nations Conference on Trade and Development (UNCTAD), said the virus outbreak could cost the global economy up to $ 2 trillion this year and that the pandemic could cause a recession in some countries causing global economic growth to clock in between 2.5 % . The Indian government is facing the twin challenge of containing the virus when the economy is already in the slowdown.

On 24 March 2020, the government of India under Prime Minister Narendra Modi ordered a nationwide lockdown for 21 days, limiting movement of the entire 1.3 billion population of India as a preventive measure towards the 2020 coronavirus pandemic in India. It was ordered after a 14 hour voluntary public curfew on 22 nd March 2020, followed by enforcement of a series of regulations in the country's COVID-19 affected regions.

The lockdown restricts people from stepping out of their homes. All transport services – road, air and rail were suspended with exceptions for transportation of essential goods, fire, police and emergency services. Educational institutions, industrial establishments and hospitality services were also suspended. Services such as food shops, banks and ATMs, petrol pumps, other essentials and their manufacturing are exempted. The Home Ministry said that anyone who fails to follow the restrictions can face up to a year in jail.

As soon as the announcement of lockdown was made, people across the country resorted to panic buying to stock essentials despite Prime Minister's assurance of their supply. Amazon India and Flipkart temporarily suspended their services after the lockdown. Food delivery schemes were banned by several state governments despite central government's approval. Thousands of people emigrated out of major Indian cities, as they became jobless after the lockdown.

Henk Bekedam, WHO representative to India praised the response describing it as "timely, comprehensive and robust." WHO executive director, Mike Ryan said that lockdowns alone will not eliminate coronavirus. He said that India must take necessary measures to prevent the second and third wave of infections.

CHAPTER SEVEN

CONCLUSION

The present situation in India is quite hopeful. India has a lot of talented people. The Universities and Educational Institutions in India are improving.

India has also taken several other steps like National Institution for Transforming India (NITI) Aayog, Pradhan Mantri AawasYojona etc.

At present Narendra Modi is trying to transform India into a digital India. Under the leadership of Modi, India is on its way to become a superpower in the near future. India also deserves a permanent seat in the United Nations Security Council.

Today India is the fourth largest military power in the world and is also the fourth largest military contributor to the United Nations Peace Keeping Force. India has also made regular financial contribution to the UN.

www.ingramcontent.com/pod-product-compliance
Lightning Source LLC
Chambersburg PA
CBHW021200130726
47988CB00004B/1701